WIT & WISDOM FOR THE

WORKPLACE

···

A LITTLE SURVIVAL GUIDE
FOR LIFE ON THE JOB

by todd & jedd hafer

© 2015 by Elevate

Editorial Content: AnnaMarie McHargue

Cover Designer: Mark Voss Design

Interior Layout: Mark Voss Design

© 2016 by Todd Hafer and Jedd Hafer

Published by Elevate, a division of Elevate Publishing, Boise, ID

ISBN: 9781943425143

wit & wisdom for the

WORKPLACE

A LITTLE SURVIVAL GUIDE
FOR LIFE ON THE JOB

by todd & jedd hafer

elevate

I always arrive late
at the office, but I make
up for it by leaving early.

charles lamb

On the job. It's where you spend the lion's share of your waking hours. Maybe a few of your slumbering hours as well, especially if the boss likes to give long PowerPoint presentations. Many people spend more time at the job than they do with their families, enjoying leisure pursuits, or snoozing contentedly in their beds.

Consider this: if you began a full-time job at age 22 and will retire at 65, you will spend the equivalent of 3,440 24-hour days on the job. That's 9.5 round-the-clock years of nothing but work. No vacations, holidays, or sick time. Most likely, these numbers will be even higher for you, esteemed reader. You're better than average, but that means you work harder than average.

According to the Gallup organization, America's small-business owners work 52 hours a week. Fifty-seven percent of them work six days a week. More than a quarter of this group work at least 60 hours every week. Seventy percent regularly work weekends.

And, according to an ABC report, 32 percent of ALL American workers toil more than 45 hours a week – more than 1,800 hours every year. America works longer than any other industrialized nation, including Germany, Great Britain, and Japan.

Our jobs are, at once, an incredible sacrifice and an incredible investment. That's why it's so important to glean as much wisdom, joy, skill, and satisfaction as you can.

This book is designed to help you do just that. You work hard. You deserve a book that works for you. We hope you're holding it right now.

Jedd and Todd Hafer

WORKPLACE MAXIM

If you are good,
you will be assigned all the work.
If you are really good,
you will get out of it.

IF AT FIRST YOUR
COMMITTEE DOES NOT
SUCCEED . . .
FORM A NEW COMMITTEE
WITH A FANCIER NAME.

DREW CODY

SIGN SEEN
ON OFFICE DOOR

Please keep your voice down;

I'm trying to sleep.

WORKPLACE TIP:

No matter how tempting,
don't check your email or
text messages during meetings.
Daydream about golf or
lounging on the beach instead.
Give the meeting leader and
the other attendees the
illusion that they have
your full attention.

Signs You're Working Too Hard

- You try to enter your computer password on the microwave oven.

- You have not played Solitaire with real cards in years.

- When calling from your home phone, you instinctively dial 9 to get an outside line.

- You email your spouse to ask if he/she wants to watch TV with you.

Trust yourself.
You know more
than you think.

dr. benjamin spock

Workplace Maxim

Your co-workers will forget
much of what you say,
but they will remember
almost everything you do.

For God so
loved the world,
that He did not
send a committee.

rev. robert st. john

WORKPLACE IMPONDERABLE

Can the boss give a speech
so boring that even he can't
stay awake through it?

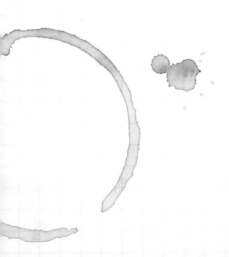

Workplace Maxim

What hits the fan
will NOT be
evenly distributed.

MAN DOES NOT
LIVE BY
GNP ALONE.

PAUL SAMUELSON

WORKPLACE MAXIM

Never plan a two-day vacation.
It takes at least two days
just to forget about work.

If you're not nervous, you're not paying attention.

miles davis

HUMILITY

is not thinking less of yourself;
it is thinking of yourself less.

rick warren

Workplace Imponderable:

Why are so many presentations touting the latest technology marred by technical difficulties?

Signs You Need
Human Resources Counseling
for Your Coffee "Problem"

• You refer to your co-workers as your "coffee mates."

• You gargle with coffee-flavored mouthwash.

• You can often be found in the break room playing
 Ping Pong. Without an opponent.

• You don't tan; you roast.

• You can't wait to go to bed each night,
 just so you can "wake up and smell the coffee."

Don't worry too much about being punctual on the job. Usually, there's no one there to appreciate it.

george house

SUCCESS IS A LOUSY TEACHER.

IT SEDUCES SMART PEOPLE

INTO THINKING THEY CAN'T LOSE.

bill gates

What the world really needs is more love and less paperwork.

pearl bailey

WORKPLACE TIP

When microwaving food,
make sure you don't over-microwave.
The aroma of burnt popcorn,
for example, doesn't enhance
anyone's workday.

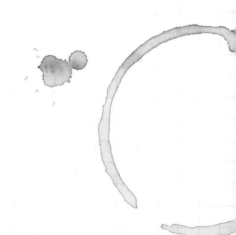

STAY ALERT
YOU CAN OBSERVE
A LOT BY WATCHING.

yogi berra

Workplace Maxim

When you forgive a co-worker
for a mistake, you make
two people feel a lot better.

HARD WORK

never killed anybody,
but why take a chance?

edgar bergen

Lampner's Law of Employment

When you work late,
you will go unnoticed.
When you leave work early,
you will meet the boss
in the parking lot.

A filing cabinet is where you can lose things systematically.

t.h. thompson

Workplace Maxim

One outstanding criterion
for measuring your job success
is the number of people
you've made happy.

Did you know?

In a recent CareerBuilders survey, 20 percent of American workers confessed to being late to work at least once a week.

WORKPLACE TIP

When conversing with co-workers,
never underestimate the power
of eye contact and a
sincere smile.

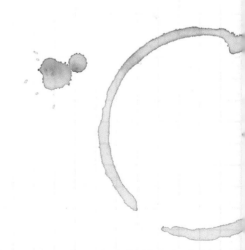

A WORKING-CLASS HERO
IS SOMETHING TO BE.

john lennon

Workplace Imponderable:

If employees are supposed to remember what's in the Policy Manual, why didn't the people who wrote it use language that one can actually understand?

More Signs You Need
Human Resources Counseling
for Your Coffee "Problem"

- The main reason you have a job is for the coffee breaks.

- To you, being called a "drip" is a compliment.

- You named your cats Cream and Sugar.

- You have lobbied to have Juan Valdez declared a saint.

- Your face is on the Colombian postage stamp.

- Your computer password is ARABICA

The office optimist
is the person who
always believes that
the meeting
will end early.

drew cody

WORKPLACE MAXIM

It is better to be divided by truth than to be united by error.

SUCCESS

is often nothing more than moving
from one failure to the next
with undiminished ethusiasm.

winston churchill

IF EVOLUTION
REALLY WORKS,
WHY DOES MY
SECRETARY HAVE
ONLY TWO HANDS?

REV. JERRY SPRINGSTON

Workplace Maxim

If you don't think
little things mean a lot at work,
just try paying attention
in a meeting when there's a
fly buzzing around the room.

The best time to give your employees advice is after they're first hired—when they are still naïve enough to believe you know what you're talking about.

h.j. springston

Workplace Maxim

Find a job you love,
and you'll never have to
work a day in your life.

Some people drink
at the fountain
of knowledge.
Others just gargle.

american proverb

My boss has two secretaries, a thousand-dollar watch, and the most expensive PDA on the market. And he hasn't been on time to a meeting in three years.

todd hafer

I ♥ DEADLINES.

*I like the whooshing sound
they make as they fly by.*

douglas adams

WORKPLACE MAXIM

A rumor can travel all
the way around the company
and back again while the truth
is still putting on its socks.

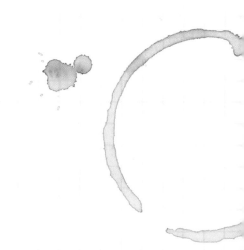

Did you know?

According to a survey
commissioned by Cisco Systems,
nearly half of all workplace
data-loss incidents result
from employees downloading
unauthorized programs
on their work computers.

Retirement at 65 is ridiculous. When I was 65, I still had pimples.

george burns

Workplace Maxim

While traveling on business,
don't kill yourself to get
down to the baggage carousel.
The first piece of luggage
it spits out never seems to
belong to anyone!

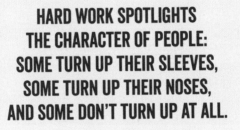

HARD WORK SPOTLIGHTS
THE CHARACTER OF PEOPLE:
SOME TURN UP THEIR SLEEVES,
SOME TURN UP THEIR NOSES,
AND SOME DON'T TURN UP AT ALL.

sam ewing

IF YOU THINK IT'S HARD
TO MEET PEOPLE AS A
NEW EMPLOYEE, JUST TRY
GRABBING SOMEONE ELSE'S
LUNCH OUT OF THE BREAK-
ROOM REFRIGERATOR.

JEDD HAFER

Workplace Maxim

The more you speak kindly
to your colleagues,
the easier it gets.

You can get by
on charm for about
fifteen minutes.
After that, you better
know something.

h. jackson brown jr.

I like work.
It fascinates me.
I can sit and look
at it for hours.

jerome k. jerome

You know it's time to consider retirement when . . .

- You sit in a rocking chair, but you can't get it started.

- Your idea of weight-lifting is standing up after a long meeting.

- Your boss regularly compliments you on your patience, but you know the secret is that you just don't care anymore.

I'm so insecure
these days that I'm
using staples on my
Post-It notes.

patrick t. stallman

I HAVEN'T SPOKEN
TO MY BOSS IN YEARS.
I DON'T WANT TO
INTERRUPT HIM.

george house

Workplace Tip

When mistakes happen,
try to take more than
your share of the blame.
When successes happen,
try to give others more than
their share of the credit.

Accomplishing the impossible means only that the boss will add it to your regular duties.

doug larson

WORKPLACE TIP

Even though it might take
a bite out of your busy day,
try to attend co-workers' birthday
and employment-anniversary
celebrations. Your presence will
be noted (as would your absence).

Possible Excuses to Use if You Get Caught Sleeping on the Job

"When I donated all that blood to save all those lives yesterday, they told me this might happen."

"Someone must have put decaf in the coffee maker this morning."

"I wasn't sleeping; I was just deeply meditating on the boss' recent pep talk."

"Wow. The 15-minute power nap recommended by Human Resources really works!"

". . . and bless my beloved fellow employees. In God's name, amen."

O, how full of
briars is the
working-day world!

william shakespeare

Did you know?

According to a survey commissioned by Cisco Systems, 63 percent of employees use their work computers for personal reasons every day.

I have found that if you love your job, your job will love you back.

rev. jerry springston

Did you Know?

People who do a lot of
business driving can become
over-dependent on GPS devices.
Psychiatrists recommend being
aware of one's overall environment-
having a big picture assessment of
where something (a company, hotel,
or conference center) is located.

THE UNIFORMS AT MY JOB
MAKE EVERYONE LOOK THE
SAME YOUNG AND OLD, SHORT
AND TALL ALIKE. HOWEVER,
IS "BAD" A GOOD THING
TO HAVE IN COMMON?

DREW CODY

WORKPLACE MAXIM

If you find yourself wondering,
"Is this outfit appropriate
for work," the answer is "NO!"

My job is going great. I have enough money to last me the rest of my life—unless I buy something.

jackie mason

OPPORTUNITY

*is missed by most people because it is
dressed in overalls and looks like work*

thomas edison

WORKPLACE IMPONDERABLE:

Are Mondays really days
that the Lord hath made?
(And if so, why hath He?)

SUCCESSES MIGHT INSPIRE A BUSINESS, BUT FAILURES MATURE A BUSINESS.

rev. robert st. john

THE BEST THING ABOUT MY HOME OFFICE? THE COMMUTE.

drew cody

Did you know?

According to the
website JustJobs.com,
20 percent of Americans
lie or exaggerate
on their résumés.

The Procrastinator's Creed

I believe that
if anything is worth doing,
it would have
been done already.

A well-developed sense of humor is the pole that adds balance to your steps as you walk the tightrope of life.

william a. ward

I've had really bad luck with administrative assistants. My first two quit on me, and the third one didn't.

constance rivers

SEARCH ALL YOUR PARKS
IN ALL YOUR CITIES;
YOU'LL FIND NO STATUES
OF COMMITTEES..

DAVID OGILVY

Did you know?

Several surveys have isolated the three most important qualities people want in a co-worker:

Trustworthiness
Loyalty
Attentive listening

FAILURE IS
THE OPPORTUNITY
TO BEGIN AGAIN—
MORE INTELLIGENTLY.

henry ford

NOTABLE CAREER CHANGES

Gerald R. Ford
a model turned U.S. President

Dean Martin
a steel worker turned entertainer

Golda Meir
a school teacher turned prime minister

Howard Cosell
an attorney turned broadcaster

Tim Green
an NFL lineman turned novelist and attorney

Babe Ruth
a bartender turned baseball player

There is absolutely no substitute for a genuine lack of preparation.

american proverb

WORKPLACE MAXIM

When you take a long time
to do something, you are slow.
When your boss takes a long time,
he or she is just being thorough.

Well done is better than well said.

ben franklin

Workplace Maxim

Good Idea:
Dressing for the next job
up the ladder.

Bad Idea:
Spending money as if
you already have the next
job up the ladder.

THOSE WHO CAN, DO;
THOSE WHO CANNOT START
GIVING SEMINARS ON
HOW TO DO IT.

PURIM

Workplace Maxim

If you don't govern your temper
on the job, your temper will
start to govern you.

Remember, if people
talk behind your back,
it only means you are two
steps ahead.

fannie flagg

WORKPLACE MAXIM

If you're debating whether
to forward that hilarious joke,
pdf, or video clip, there's
probably a very good reason
for your hesitation.

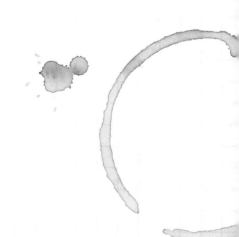

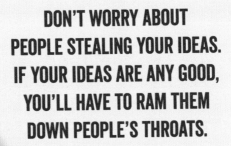

DON'T WORRY ABOUT
PEOPLE STEALING YOUR IDEAS.
IF YOUR IDEAS ARE ANY GOOD,
YOU'LL HAVE TO RAM THEM
DOWN PEOPLE'S THROATS.

howard aiken

ALL WORK, EVEN COTTON SPINNING, IS NOBLE.

thomas carlyle

NOTABLE CAREER CHANGES (PART 2)

Boris Karloff
a realtor turned horror-flick actor

Clark Gable
a lumberjack turned actor

Paul Gauguin
a stockbroker turned artist

Steve Martin
a magician turned comedian

Albert Einstein
a patent-office clerk turned physicist

Mike Reid
a pro football player turned country-music star

CREATIVITY

is allowing yourself to make mistakes.
Art is knowing which ones to keep.

scott adams,
creator of "dilbert"

You know you're entrenched in corporate America when . . .

- You refer to your family as "my team-based organization."

- Your Valentine's Day cards feature bullet points.

- You mark each wedding anniversary with a detailed performance review.

- You refer to marrying off one of your kids as "right-sizing."

- You end every personal argument by saying, "Let's take this offline."

The supreme accomplishment is to blur the line between work and play.

arnold toynbee

WORKPLACE MAXIM

Never do anything
too memorable at the
company Christmas party.

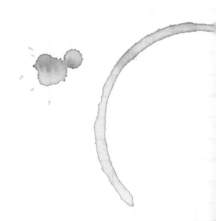

Brilliance is like
four-wheel drive:
It enables a person
to get stuck in even more
remote places.

garrison keillor

ALL NATURE
SEEMS
AT WORK.

SAMUEL TAYLOR

I do not like
work even when
another person
does it.

mark twain

Workplace Maxim

The boss always has two
reasons for a policy change:
a good reason and the real reason.

I AM THE PEOPLE.
DO YOU KNOW THAT ALL
THE GREAT WORK OF THE WORLD
IS DONE THROUGH ME?

carl sandburg

Start every day off with a smile and get it over with.

w.c. fields

WORKPLACE MAXIM

In a business meeting,
when someone says,
"To make a long story short . . ."
it's too late.

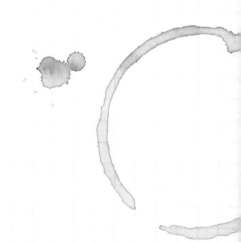

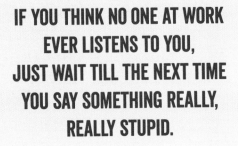

IF YOU THINK NO ONE AT WORK
EVER LISTENS TO YOU,
JUST WAIT TILL THE NEXT TIME
YOU SAY SOMETHING REALLY,
REALLY STUPID.

todd hafer

WE PRETEND TO WORK BECAUSE THEY PRETEND TO PAY US.

russian proverb

Workplace Tip

Don't think twice
before sending a critical email
to (or about) someone.
Think at least three times!

At my last job,
the cafeteria served
nothing but leftovers
for years. No one could
recall the original meal
ever being served!

george house

Workplace Maxim

There is no such thing
as a minor lapse
of integrity.

10 Keys to Work Success

1. Believe when others doubt.
2. Learn while others loaf.
3. Decide while others delay.
4. Begin while others procrastinate.
5. Work while others wish.
6. Save while others spend.
7. Listen while others talk.
8. Smile while others scowl.
9. Compliment while others criticize.
10. Persist when others quit.

WORK IS LIKE LIFE;
BOTH ARE MUCH MORE
INTERESTING IF YOU
DON'T HAVE ALL THE
ANSWERS..

H.J. SPRINGSTON

Workplace Maxim

If you must refer to
a colleague as a real asset,
pronounce your words carefully.

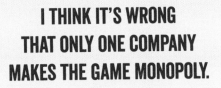

I THINK IT'S WRONG
THAT ONLY ONE COMPANY
MAKES THE GAME MONOPOLY.

steven wright

WORKPLACE MAXIM

Teamwork means never
having to take all
the blame yourself.

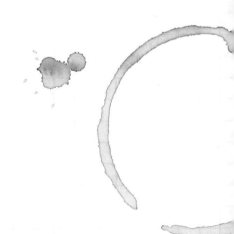

You can send a message around the world in one-seventh of a second, yet it might take years to force a simple idea through a quarter-inch of a human skull.

charles f. kettering

Workplace Maxim

When you do something without being told, you're overstepping your authority. When the boss does it, it's showing initiative.

IMAGINATION
is more important than knowledge.

albert einstein

NOTABLE CAREER CHANGES (PART 3)

Sean Connery
bricklayer and trucker turned actor

Johnny Carson
magician turned talk show host

Desi Arnaz
birdcage cleaner turned band leader/actor

Rich Franklin
math teacher turned world-champion
mixed-martial-arts fighter

Vitali Klitschko
boxing champion turned Mayor of Kiev

Did you know?

According to the online newsletter Career Copilot, here are the five work benefits that employees value most:

- Health insurance
- Paid vacation
- Dental insurance
- A 401K plan
- Bonuses

An idea can turn
to dust or magic,
depending on the talent
that rubs against it.

william bernbach

The brain is a wonderful organ. It starts working the moment you get up in the morning, and does not stop until you get into the office.

robert frost

Signs You're Working Too Hard

1. You find yourself highlighting portions of a restaurant menu.

2. You find yourself entering your employee number on the TV remote.

3. Even your love letters contain bullet points and outlines.

4. When you talk in your sleep, you recite passages from the Employment Manual.

5. The company just named a conference room after you.

YOU WIN A FEW,
YOU LOSE A FEW.
SOME GET RAINED OUT.
BUT YOU GOT TO DRESS
FOR ALL OF THEM.

satchel paige
hall of fame baseball player

THE BOSS WHO LAUGHS
WITH HIS EMPLOYEES
MORE THAN HE LECTURES
THEM IS WAY AHEAD
OF THE GAME.

rev. jerry springston

*A Sign Seen on an
Office Bulletin Board*

Of course
I don't look busy.
I did it right
the first time!

Success and failure
are greatly overrated.
But failure gives you
a whole lot more to
talk about.

hildegard knef

IF AT FIRST YOU
DON'T SUCCEED...
TRY UPPER MANAGEMENT.

george house

WORKPLACE MAXIM

An office memo lies somewhere
between an official document
and a perfectly good blank
sheet of paper.

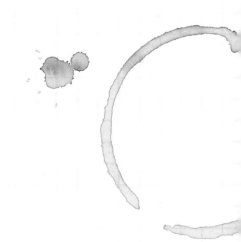

I do marathons.
I do meetings.
I do not do
marathon meetings.

todd hafer

About the only problem with success is that it does not teach you how to deal with failure.

tommy lasorda, champion baseball manager

I PAID FOR MY COFFEE WITH A TWENTY, AND THE BARISTA ASKED IF I HAD ANYTHING SMALLER. I WAS TEMPTED TO SAY, "MY PAYCHECK?"

jedd hafer

Workplace Maxim

Always give the boss
time to collect his thoughts.
Both of them.

Thinking is the hardest work there is, which is probably the reason so few engage in it.

henry ford

Workplace Tip

In a meeting, be careful
about criticizing an idea.
That idea's author might be
in the room with you!

SUCCESS
is often just an idea away.

frank tyger

Workplace Maxim

Procrastination is the art
of keeping up with yesterday.

**Always do right.
This will gratify some
and astonish the rest.**

mark twain

Irrefutable Business Truths

1. A clear conscience should never be confused with a faulty memory.

2. A closed mouth gathers no foot.

3. Invoices travel at twice the speed of checks.

4. It is better to light one small candle than be seen under fluorescent lighting with no makeup.

Workplace Maxim

If you're wondering,
"Should I visit the bathroom
before the upcoming meeting?"
the answer is YES!

IT'S KIND OF FUN TO DO THE IMPOSSIBLE.

walt disney

WORKPLACE MAXIM

To get the best out of
your co-workers, you must look
for the best that is in them.

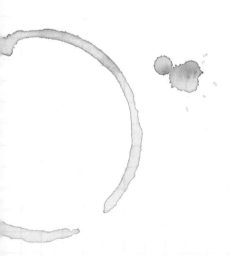

How far you go in life
depends on your being
tender with the young,
compassionate with the aged,
sympathetic with the striving,
and tolerant of the weak
and the strong. Because
someday in life you will have
been all of these.

george washington carver

Did you know?

Being nervous about a big
presentation can cause errors
in judgment. If you find yourself
stressing before facing the big
bosses and your co-workers,
give yourself a few minutes
to collect your thoughts and pray
or meditate to quiet your heart.

THE BEGINNING
IS THE MOST
IMPORTANT PART
OF THE WORK.

PLATO

Workplace Maxim

If at first
you DO succeed...
try not to look
so astonished.

10 Things to MAKE at Work—Besides Money

1. Time
2. Merry
3. Do
4. Up
5. Sense
6. Peace
7. Room
8. Waves
9. Amends
10. Believe

I'm a self-made man,
but if I had to do
it all over again,
I would outsource
the job.

roland young

You know it's time to consider retirement when . . .

- You try to straighten out the wrinkles in your socks—then realize you aren't wearing socks.

- Even when you stay home, your back goes out.

- Getting ready for work, it takes you twice as long to look half as good.

- Most of the names of your LinkedIn contacts start with "Dr."

BY THE WORK
ONE KNOWS
THE WORKMAN.

jean de la fontaine

Workplace Maxim

The worker who
smiles in the face
of adversity . . .
probably has a
handy scapegoat.

No vacation
goes unpunished.

karl a. hakkarainen

**Procrastination means
you know what you need to do,
but you don't do it.
If you don't know what to do, you
are not procrastinating.
You are thinking.**

lynn lively

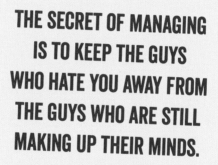

THE SECRET OF MANAGING
IS TO KEEP THE GUYS
WHO HATE YOU AWAY FROM
THE GUYS WHO ARE STILL
MAKING UP THEIR MINDS.

casey stengel,
legendary baseball manager

Why do vacation days
seem to pass at twice
the speed of workdays?

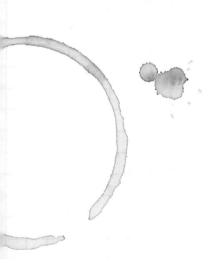

WHATEVER YOU CAN DO
OR DREAM YOU CAN,
BEGIN IT. BOLDNESS
HAS BEAUTY, POWER,
AND MAGIC IN IT..

JOHANN WOLFGANG VON GOETHE

We have too much to do, thanks to a digital culture that creates the illusion that we can get more done in the same amount of time.

william powers, **author of** *Hamlet's Blackberry: Building A Good Life in the Digital Age*

Workplace Maxim

No day on the job
is so bad that it can't
be fixed with a nap!

To be clever enough
to get all the money,
one must be stupid
enough to want it.

g.k. chesterton

The most important part of being a salesperson is confidence. Confidence is like going after Moby Dick with a rowboat, a harpoon, and a jar of tartar sauce.

robert orben

WORKPLACE MAXIM

Even in these high-tech times,
the suggestion box is a good idea.
(Anything employees have to say should
be kept under lock and key.)

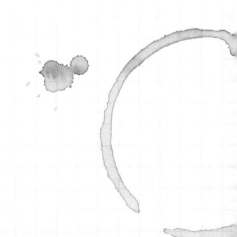

THE OLDER I GET,
THE BETTER I USED TO BE.

lee trevino

Office Beatitude

Blessed are you when
you have little stumbles,
for they prevent big falls.

WORKPLACE MAXIM

The Human Resources folks
are probably NOT
secretly monitoring all of your
phone calls and emails.
You should behave,
however, as if they are.

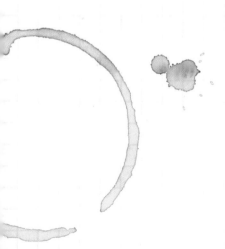

**Those who say
it cannot be done
should not interrupt
the person doing it.**

chinese proverb

You know it's time to consider retirement when . . .

- It takes you longer to rest up than it did to get tired.

- The only birthday gift you want from your co-workers is NOT to be reminded of your age.

- At the breakfast table before work, you hear lots of Snap! Crackle! and Pop! But you aren't eating cereal.

- When crouching to tie your shoe, you look around for something else to accomplish while you're down there.

Common sense is genius dressed up in work clothes.

ralph waldo emerson

IF YOU WANT TO KNOW
WHAT GOD THINKS OF MONEY,
JUST LOOK AT THE PEOPLE
HE GAVE IT TO.

dorothy parker

Workplace Maxim

People who listen
to office gossip
deserve to be lied to.

IF EVERYTHING
IS UNDER CONTROL,
YOU ARE GOING
TOO SLOW.

**mario andretti,
legendary race-car driver**

All work and no play makes Jack a dull boy.

james howell

EXPERIENCE
is the name everyone gives their mistakes.

oscar wilde

Workplace Maxim

Beware when things
are going great you might
have overlooked something.

Workplace Tip

If you find yourself
habitually late for meetings,
don't put meeting start-times
into your calendar, phone,
or daily planner.
Put the time you need
to leave for each meeting.

To love what you do
and feel that it matters—
how could anything
be more fun?

katharine graham

Every day, I get up and
look through the
Forbes list of the
richest people in America.
If I'm not there,
I go to work

robert orben

Workplace
Signs of the Times

(actual signs from businesses around the world)

On a dance-club marquee:
**Smarts is the most exclusive club
in town. Everyone is welcome!**

Notice in a dry cleaner's window:
**Anyone leaving their garments here for
more than 30 days will be disposed of!**

Notice in a health-food shop window:
Closed due to illness.

On a repair-shop door:
**We fix anything! (Please knock hard
on the door – the bell doesn't work.)**

Note on a washroom in a London office building:
**Toilet out of order.
Please use floor below.**

Workplace Maxim

Concerns about the problem
of too many emails and
office memos should not
be expressed via an email
or office memo.

If a train station
is where the
train stops,
what's a
workstation?

author unknown

According to most studies,
people's number one fear
is public speaking.
Number two is death.
Death is number two!
Does that sound right?
That means, to the average person,
if you go to a funeral,
you're better off in the casket
than doing the eulogy.

jerry seinfeld

Even if you're
on the right track,
you'll get nowhere
if you just sit there.

will rogers

International business travel tip:

If you actually look like
your passport photo,
you're way too sick to travel.

THE ROAD
TO SUCCESS
IS ALWAYS
UNDER
CONSTRUCTION.

JIM MILLER

A FEW THINGS THEY PROBABLY DIDN'T TEACH YOU IN BUSINESS SCHOOL

- Never test the depths of the water with both feet.

- If you tell the truth, you don't have to remember so much.

- If you lend a co-worker 20 bucks and never see that person again, it was probably worth it.

- Never underestimate the power of ignorant people in large committees.

- Good judgment comes from bad experiences, and many of those bad experiences come from having really bad judgment.

- Never miss a good chance to shut up.

- Office diplomacy is the art of saying "nice doggie" while looking for a big stick.

- The older you get, the better you get (unless you're a banana).

SIGN SEEN
ON OFFICE DOOR

I'm out of my mind
but feel free to leave a message.

**Many people
quit looking for work
when they find a job.**

american proverb

A lot of fellows nowadays
have a B.A., M.D., or Ph.D.
Unfortunately, they do not
have a J.O.B.

fats domino

WORKPLACE IMPONDERABLE

Why is the person who
tries to solve a problem
the one who ends up getting
blamed for creating it?

t.s. eliot

Just Another Day at the Office
My assistant is out sick today,
The printer's out of toner.
My car is in the shop again,
I'm forced to drive a loaner.

Two new software programs to learn,
But the verbiage makes me dizzy.
I've tried to summon tech support,
But their line is always busy.

The repairman's mangled the copier,
So my report will be quite late.
With people buzzing round like flies,
How can I concentrate?

My phone is buzzing endlessly,
There's gossip in the halls.
My candy dish is empty now,
and a sales rep's come to call.

Sometimes I'd like to chuck it all,
Trade this madness in for boredom.
But the kids need braces, clothes, and shoes,
How else can I afford 'em?

Workplace
Signs of the Times

(actual signs from businesses around the world)

In a London department store:
Bargain Basement Upstairs.

Outside a farm supply store:
Horse manure – five dollars pre-packed, two dollars do-it-yourself!

Outside a second-hand shop:
We exchange anything – bicycles, washing machines, etc. Why not bring your wife along and get a wonderful bargain?

Outside a town hall in Britain:
The town hall is closed until opening. It will remain closed after being opened. Open tomorrow.

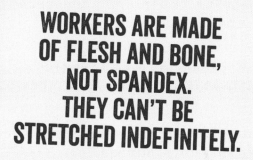

WORKERS ARE MADE OF FLESH AND BONE, NOT SPANDEX. THEY CAN'T BE STRETCHED INDEFINITELY.

h.j. springston

WHY YOU SHOULD PROOF-READ YOUR RESUME
("GREATEST MISSES" FROM RESUMES AND JOB APPLICATIONS)

"I have a graduate degree in unclear physics."

"In my previous position, I saved the company $29K a year by removing ornamental pants from the reception area and the cafeteria."

"My previous job was serving as a deceptionist in a lawyer's office."

"My architectural experience includes designing golf curses."

"I worked for twelve years as an uninformed security guard."

"My volunteer experience includes delivering hot males to senior citizens."

"I left my previous job because my souse is in the Army and had to relocate."

"I desire to work for a company that promotes Judo-Christian values."

"My last job was assistant manager at Walters Plumbing and Hating."

"The academic scholarship I earned came with a $5,000 award and a plague."

"Most of my experience at this point has been as a blue-color worker."

"As part of the city-maintenance crew, I repaired bad roads and defective brides."

"My career goal is to shave my talents with a growing business."

"My hobbies include raising long-eared rabbis as pets."

Lazy hands make a man poor, but diligent hands bring wealth.

proverbs 10:4

Did you know?

Walt Disney was fired
from a newspaper job
because he lacked ideas.
Later, he went bankrupt
several times before he built
Disneyland and created
Disney Studios.

12 Irrefutable Pearls of Business Wisdom

- Before you criticize co-workers, walk a mile in their shoes.
  That way, if they get angry, they will be a mile away, and barefoot.

- It is almost always easier to get forgiveness than permission.

- For every action, there is an equal and opposite management
  policy to hinder it.

- Age is a very high price to pay for wisdom and maturity.

- Middle management is the point at which broadness of the mind
  and narrowness of the waist change places.

- Opportunities always look bigger going than arriving.

- "Office Junk" is something you throw away two weeks before
  you desperately need it.

- At any job, there is always one more imbecile than you counted on.

- Artificial intelligence is no match for natural stupidity.

- Experience is a wonderful thing: It enables you to recognize
  a mistake when you make it again.

- By the time your small business can make ends meet,
  someone moves the ends!

- Blessed are those who can laugh at their own mistakes,
  for they shall never cease to be amused.

Money
never made
anyone rich.

seneca

Ah, Corporate Suburbia, where they rip out the trees, then name streets after them.

george house

*A Sign Seen on an
Office Bulletin Board*

Well, this day was
a TOTAL waste of makeup.

WHERE OUR
WORK IS,
THERE LET
OUR JOY BE.

TERTULLIAN